Hello from Montaque

Our approach is founded in the strong belief that mindfulness has the power to lower stress, reduce anxiety, and increase a sense of wellness. We hope you enjoy spending time with the unique nature scenes, mandala and stained glass patterns, and mindfulness poems that we specially created for this book.

If you'd like to receive free additional coloring pages, please visit us at:

www.montaquebooks.com

Mindful Nature
Adult Coloring Book

Take a moment to breathe
Listen to the air fill up your lungs
Feel your chest expand
When you release,
Let go.

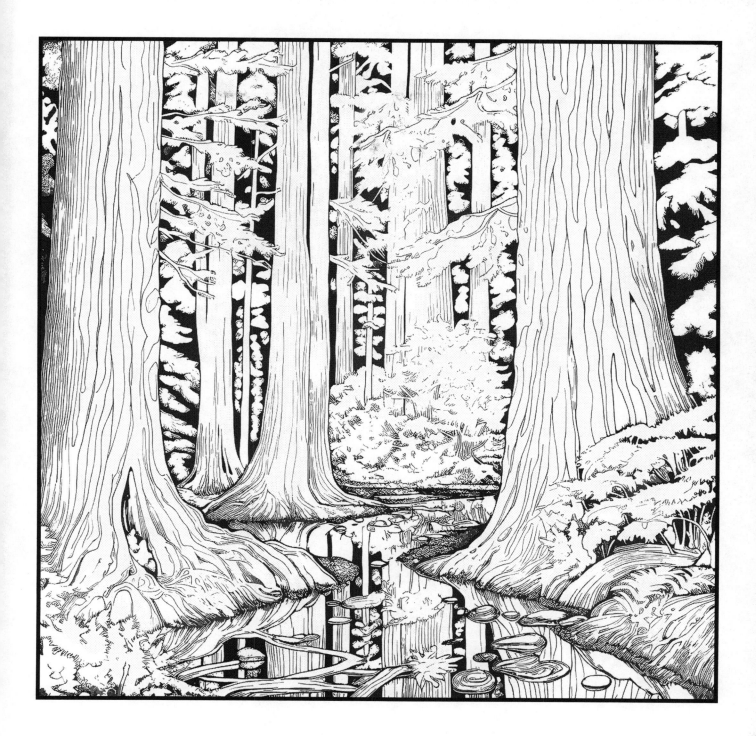

Nature vs nurture:
Why not have both?
When we nurture nature,
Nature nurtures us too.

Recipe for grounding yourself:
Start by expressing gratitude
Add a helping of forgiveness
Mix in a dash of self–love
And sit for 10 minutes at room
temperature.

Focus on the present
What do you hear?
What do you see?
When you pay attention to the "now"
You receive the gift of mindfulness

The mind is like the surface of the ocean
It can be calm and serene
Or stormy and tumultuous
Yet, no matter its state
The eternal You swims freely
Deep below its depths

Made in the USA
Columbia, SC
28 December 2024

50717110R00063